FOR YOU, I WILL

ELLE DUNCAN

ILLUSTRATED BY **LAURA FREEMAN**

&

ANDSCAPE

Disney · HYPERION

Los Angeles   New York

To my daughter, Eva Rose,
who has opened my eyes and heart in ways I never dreamed.
Seek the light or serve as it, just never stop shining, baby girl.
—E.D.

For my sons, Griffin and Milo, who fill my heart with love
—L.F.

First Edition, March 2024
10 9 8 7 6 5 4 3 2 1
FAC-025393-23332
Printed in China

This book is set in Flanders/Fontspring
Designed by Joann Hill
Illustrations created digitally

Library of Congress Control Number: 2022059448
ISBN 978-1-368-08367-6
Reinforced binding
Visit www.AndscapeBooks.com and www.DisneyBooks.com

I will wrap my arms around you so you will know comfort.

I will stand steady while you find your footing.
I'll walk tall while you find your stride.

For you, I will.

When you speak about your
goals, joys, and fears, I will listen

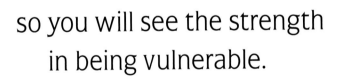

so you will see the strength
in being vulnerable.

In a world that would
try to quiet you
and attempt to dim
your flame,

RIGHTS

I will help you find your voice
to be bold and unafraid.

I'll take on that load for you
so you can pack light.

Fly, baby girl.
For you, I will.

Self-care is not selfish.
You can be giving and kind to others
and to yourself.

For you, I will shine
and I will lead,
passionately, humbly, joyfully,
so that you will approach
your purpose the same way.

Let the sway of my hips,
the strength in my step,
the tilt of my chin
be your guide.

We will celebrate our differences.
You are unique and a part of
a beautiful community.

We don't simply
accept the skin we're in,
we rejoice in it!

I will teach you about your ancestors,
their stories and triumphs,
so you will know that
you are born of titans!

Built for pressure,
made to last.

But most importantly, my sweet girl,
I will play with you.

We will laugh.

I will wear my joy like the fitted crown of a queen
so that you will radiate like the glow of a thousand stars.

And when you're ready to leave,
I'll be brave enough to let you go.

Burning bright in every dark space,
through any tough moment,
you will be the light
and I your faithful spark.

I will make it my life's mission.

For you, I will.

TITANS OF

BILLIE HOLIDAY
Jazz singer

BESSIE COLEMAN
Pilot

MADAM C. J. WALKER
Entrepreneur, philanthropist,
and activist

FANNIE LOU HAMER
Community organizer,
activist, and civil rights
leader

BEYONCÉ
Singer, songwriter, and
businesswoman

HISTORY

SHIRLEY CHISHOLM
Politician and activist

ELLA BAKER
Activist

IDA B. WELLS
Journalist, educator, and
civil rights leader

ROSA PARKS
Activist

SOJOURNER TRUTH
Abolitionist and activist